Lead in the Veins

Poems

Imani M. Tafari-Ama

Lead in the Veins

Second Edition
Published 2016, 2019 by Beaten Track Publishing
First published 2011
Copyright © 2011, 2016, 2019 Imani M. Tafari-Ama, Kingston.

All rights reserved.
No part of this publication may be reproduced, stored in a retrieval system, or transmitted, in any form or by any means, without the prior permission of the publisher, nor be otherwise circulated without the publisher's prior consent in any form of binding or cover other than that in which it is published and without a similar condition including this condition being imposed on the subsequent publisher.
The moral right of the author has been asserted.

ISBN: 978 1 78645 361 7

Cover Design: Trevor Bailey

Beaten Track Publishing
Burscough. Lancashire.
www.beatentrackpublishing.com

Contents

Foreword by Mutabaruka - She Use The Pen 1

Chapter 1: Setting the Stage 5

    Whipped 7
    Cockeyed Power 9
    Truth and Reconciliation 10
    Aftermath 11
    Emancipation Gloom 12
    Dead Beat 13
    Phoenix 14
    Bleached Up 15
    Risks 16

Chapter 2: Postscripts of (Black) Male Violence 17

    Suicide 19
    Beheadings 20
    It's a Man Thing 21
    Informer 22
    Life in the Ghetto 23
    Smoke and Mirrors 24

Chapter 3: Gender and Dis-Contents — 27

    All about Eve — 29
    The In-Thing — 30
    Gender Bending — 31
    Puppetmaster — 32
    Dancehall — 33

Chapter 4: In the Throes of Love — 35

    At First Sight — 37
    Serendipity — 38
    Rebirth — 39
    Mating — 40
    Long Distance — 41
    The Morning After — 42
    Make-up — 43
    Ode to the Orchid — 44
    The Awakening — 45
    Set Love Free — 46
    Bad Man, Sexy Man — 47
    Parting — 48
    Swinging — 49
    Bare Essentials — 50
    Words out of Season — 51
    Two Steps Forward — 52
    Finale — 54
    Twist — 55

Chapter 5: Existential Philosophy ... **57**
    The Other Side ... 59
    We Want Justice ... 60
    Nostalgia ... 61
    Courage of Conviction ... 62
    Politically Correct ... 63
    Outside the Box ... 64
    Information Age ... 65
    Couplet ... 66
    With Prejudice ... 67

About the Author ... **68**

Livicated
to the Revolutionaries
in my
inner circle

Foreword by Mutabaruka - She Use The Pen

She use the pen
Like a surgeon's knife
Cutting through the pain
Removing the blood stain
That strain
The hearts of many

The poet writes
Let their be light
Let the anger turn into rays
Of hope
Who can cope
With so many social ills
Too many pills
The pain still sears

the pen is searchin
For the disease that sicken
Our mind's lines drawn
Who will remove it
The poet writes
But words will not wash away
The pain
The tears of mothers cryin
Children dyin

The poet's pen must become
The surgeon's knife
That cuts and removes
This disease
That hurts us all
The system must fall
The poets call...
To order...
Turn the boat over

Come outside
Of this box that enslaves
Our mind
Our body...
The poet writes...must write
To relieve her own pain...her anger...
The chains
of her love
The poet starts from herself
The knife cuts
Like a stick
Of authority
The poet is healed
Now she can heal others
Sick...

Mutabaruka - January 2013

Chapter 1:
Setting the Stage

As Marcus Garvey said, if we do not critically review our past, we are doomed to repeat it in the present and in the future. The pieces in this section address the pain entrenched in memories of colonialism and the lingering impact of this Holocaust on contemporary political, socio-economic and psychosocial conditions and relations shaping the lives of the progeny of enslaved Africans.

Whipped

Colonial discourses
transmute
into contemporary consumption
of exotic cultures
licensed in the name
of tourism
educational
cultural
commercial
heritage
and otherwise
sex for sale
bodies
paraded on the altar
of the almighty
dollar

brains have been washed
and like so much dirty linen
hung up on lines
and dried out
of conscious substance
the economy is the new
auction block
and debt payment transactions
require rape and plunder
of the masses
colonials and gangsters
in high and low places
sign contracts
in blood
sacrifices of humanity
for profit
and power

Cockeyed Power

In the wasteland of hypocrisy
manipulative midgets
rule the roost
cockeyed monsters
crow the dawn
a rude awakening for
hens pecking
crumbs trickle from the table
and feigning love
cackling anew
they nested on eggs
hatchlings rose triumphant
spinning a new yarn
and as they chirped
blood splattered from headlines
and headless bodies
and the feast
for Thanksgiving
began

Truth and Reconciliation

Lightning flashed
and lit the trees
left standing after
the holocaust
burning now
these trees
thought
of could-have-beens
and aborted possibilities
the wounds lay raw
undressed by
time
ignored
in space
and after the last was
razed to the ground
who dared give the signal
for healing
to begin

Aftermath

It is already too late
and
Divine intervention
may help some
but Ancestors have
so much on their plate
I weep
for the living
among us
but even more
my skin crawls
for Africa
when oppression burrows
so deep
and travels so far
across
time and space
it becomes
lead in our veins
and changes are
too few
and far between

Emancipation Gloom

Freedoms stitched
in sackcloth and ashes
piled high over bones
of equal opportunity
they eyeballed differences
while bridges creaked
under the weight of the tragedy
vultures hovered for sure pickings
as they crossed
foot soldiers looked back
at crumpled counterparts
mourning

Dead Beat

As its back broke
the camel sighed
and considered well
the last straw
it had taken
life flashed
in a mist
and he recalled
load after heavy load
grief and pain
he cried
at the waste
as he died
his master
saw his face
twitch
and the ghost of
a smile
hovering

Phoenix

Kneading wraiths of Ancestral memories
truth wells sprang to life
feeding fantasies of karmic spirits
in vain
neophytes chanted
a tortured chorus
then lay simpering
in scorched sunsets
bare now
souls searched
for common threads at
roots of ancient trees
their stirrings rendered hearts
of molten blood
stretching skins taut
over wounded lips
holding
sobs in place

Bleached Up

Skins peeling
they strut their stuff
seemingly oblivious of the
spectre they present
the setting of the sun
the signal
to emerge from cocoons
shielding
melanin-drained bodies
from searing penetration
in the cool of the night
the undertaker
got a stiff fright
no layer was left
from head to toe
to catch the seam
he used glue instead
did a patchwork job
and sealed the casket
on viewing day

Risks

Takings raked in
winnings of rare gems
and losses piled equally
high as bounty
guts spilling
they plunged buckets
well deep
and earth yieldings
sustained sanity
on the rocks

Chapter 2:
Postscripts of (Black) Male Violence

The phenomenon of Black/African male violence is a complex interweaving of the untreated trauma of African enslavement residing in the collective memory of the descendants of the millions so victimised and the failure of those responsible for this Holocaust to apologise for their moral debauchery and material oppression and exploitation, and to make amends in the form of restorative and reparative justice. The reproduction of the violent divide and rule politics by contemporary leaders; massive illiteracy among youth who have been denied access to basic human rights like food, clothing and shelter and therefore lack of choices; easy access to guns produced for profit by the world's powerful nations and denial of the connections among these elements by the powers-that-be all combine to create a vacuum. The youth use violence to fill the void, unaware of the suicidal implications of such acts of self-hate.

Suicide

He shot and killed a man
and when he heard it on the news
he smiled
at the duppy lineup
and counted eight
he had come of age
at eighteen
but when he went to sleep
that night
he dreamt he was drowning
in his own blood
and when he woke
he was choking
they say
big man don't cry
but it was a lie
he was
dying too

Beheadings

Living and dead
the ghouls hung
over the bridge
heads floated in the waters
and pan-jerked torsos
sold on Saturday night
gangster vampires
and colonial vultures
joined forces
feasts on funeral pyres
pricks for sale or hire
quagmire of trauma
festering sore points
for political pundits
no TV whodunnits
could rival the gore
trooping through
the revolving door
the masses mused we will even the score
on the table a feast
wine of astonishment bread of sorrow
priests bless flesh bone marrow
pray for truth and spirit to forgive
one last hope
live and let live

It's a Man Thing

Men make their own
misery
and when the dust settles
they leave to mourn
well-wishers
and charlatans alike
murderers mask
and mingle with
those near and dear to the dead
the tricky thing
about poverty's play
is the acts grind
to the same halt
line by line
they read
upside down
inside out
round and about
the more things change
the more they remain the same

Informer

A woman lived up the road
with two sons and a daughter
I don't know what she did
she just talked
she informed on them
and gunmen came
and shot her teeth
out of her head
and her son who was six
dived under the bed
her daughter jumped through the window
her little baby son got shot too
her big son grabbed and
threw him in the barrel
and went under the bed
when the gunmen left she was saying over and over
"Ian, Theo, Tina," her children's names
the last one she called was Ian
he got six shots but did not die right away
in the morning
when we went to look
we saw blood
and we saw teeth

Life in the Ghetto

My mother's death was a big tragedy
she was friendly with a woman
who they said
was a police informer
and the men came in the night and shot her
they killed the lady before they came
to shoot my mother because they said
that she was involved too
I was nineteen and I felt that I was going mad
I ran to the police and told them
I was going to become an officer
and kill off the gunmen
I have lived with this for years
and although it has passed and gone
and the police killed them off
I still feel it

Smoke and Mirrors

The other side of the coin
is when
people flipped it up and forgot
that the smooth side was all about
love and unity
people then started to live on the edge
and that was all about drugs, dons
guns, fast living, and corners
McWhinney Street and Stephen Lane
Raiders, Charlotte Street to Tower Street
South Camp Road and Gully Massive
Old Man Corner, Fleet Street or Renkers
Tiger Fort, Buck Town, Site, First Street, which takes in
Love in the House, Stallag 17, Super Dollar and Super Stud
Coolers, Okro Slime, Pow and Young Pow
Max and Breadfruit Tree
that's it till you reach to Tel Aviv and Spoilers
that's how the power struggle comes about
about who to run where and what
who has the most guns who is the baddest man
any one man can control here

because the man who owns his gun
is not about to take talk from another man
about what he should or should not do
because he is his own don
and that leads to death and destruction
yet all this comes from politicians
and the distribution of guns
till the so-called dons got the opportunity
of leaving and of sending
guns with the aim of arming the corners
the whole government is at a loss
as to how to solve what they call
the problems of the ghetto
where you find man and man
living on the edge
at four and five
not knowing the language to strive
to resolve the conflicts
at two and three
how can it be
that we cannot remember
how to create peace

Chapter 3:
Gender and Dis-Contents

Power differences between women and men are widely attributed to religious representations, reproduced in culture with detrimental socio-economic, psychosocial and political effects. Dismantling such dichotomies has been the preoccupation of womanists and feminists for several decades. However, despite enshrinement of freedoms in international charters, the negative impact of gender discrimination continues to provide a site of liberation struggle, in Jamaica as elsewhere in the world. This section collaborates with the cacophony of dissent.

All about Eve

In the warmth of the day
she reached out
picked an apple and waited
while whispers urged passion
and one bite later
she was hooked lined and sinkered
coming up for air
she bit and licked
her lips
delighted to taste
such sweetness
and in the cool of the day
Adam too had his way
honeyed
in sultry dusk
standing
silent and naked

The In-Thing

They ate from the tree of
knowledge of good and Eve-ill
he cursed the serpent
for aiding and abetting
to this day that phallus
is at the scene of all crimes
pointed power rules in zones of war
pricks parading cocking the
gun
sword
penis
rocket launcher
even twin towers
all tools of the same trade
vaginas on fire
and share a sheath's moniker
roots of all evil
breasts heavy with
concentrated sin
bodies at war
local and global
in God we trust
while others pay dearly
for ballistic dumping

Gender Bending

From day one we clashed
the womb conspired
our shaping
twin spirits
twin bodies
chanting delusions of grandeur
and gender bias
after birth
embodied war raged
beyond genes and hormones
social psychology
economy
and community
sacred and profane
what makes us tick
is riddled
with struggle
on highlands and low grounds
quests for morality
can't hear myself think
for the screams in
F minor
the babies sputtered
and the chants rose
to a crescendo

Puppetmaster

She turned the corner
strings tied
to aprons of her own making
no longer subject
to whims and fancies
of all and sundry
kneading her dough
of destiny
garments rent
she stood
her arching shot straight
and sure
bullseye
piercings penetrated
and she sighed
satisfied with coming
into her own

Dancehall

Dancehall is dubbed
the root of
all evil
by outside critics
while inside the space
revellers whine
and ride riddims
astonishing voyeurs
with diverse denuding
colour and clothes
stripped from bodies
laid bare
invisibility for sale
unconscious of race
careless of morality
colonising the lights
exercising agency
you'd never guess in a
passing glance
that abject poverty
is life's lot
but on second glance
it's plain to see
the thin-skinned depth
of all that beauty

Chapter 4:
In the Throes of Love

Despite their experiences of known and untold horrors, Africans in the Diaspora have created epic emotional bulwarks. Love is the constant factor that has kept mind, body and soul together and inspired the designs of strategies of survival against the odds. As torturous as it sometimes has been to navigate this road, it is the inevitable choice for foolhardy and brave alike as everyone desires - and deserves -happiness. Some find and keep it; some are momentarily touched by tantalising brushes while others search in vain for extended periods or even a lifetime. Inevitably, love's pleasure is measured in cups contoured by pain and it takes discipline to sift the gold from the dross.

At First Sight

The perfect gentleman
he held strain
against bawdy rush
of desire
and she too
restrained by convention
played safe behind the veil
till
time's fingers beckoned
heeding the call
they hastened tentative steps
sipping at love's fountain
decorously
then wild abandon set in
and boundless passion rushed
where angels
dared to tread

Serendipity

A curved ball bounced
out of left field
the game had begun
and when they were spent
the players saw serious
intent
on the linesman's flag
they had won the wager
now the deal
was on

Rebirth

Crossing stars
they alighted on cloud nine
enveloped in rose-tinted haze
moved to tears
words failed them
in the shimmering silence
they whispered sweet nothings
and mated
soul to soul
and marvelled that they
couldn't see
the woods for the trees

Mating

I never imagined that
fate would deal this hand
I still can't credit that this
fair game is my
real choice
I dipped my fingers in denial's ink
I just didn't know what to think
now faced with flashes of
Ancestral memory
I wrapped the present
in invisible packages
brewing elements of
of potlucked thoughts
and androids crossed lines
blending bodies
in steamy stews

Long Distance

From peaks to dunes
wild winds raged
charting new courses
as she wound rivers
round her fingers
in the afterglow they basked
wrapped in smiles
and delicious daydreams
hidden from the vexed eye
of the thunderstorm
scampering for cover
arm in arm with wishful thinking
they crisscrossed the prairie
coming to the edge of tomorrow
and jumped
dancing on moonbeams
and the whisper of song

The Morning After

I too
drown
in the swelling tide
taking my breath away
leaving me
at a loss for words
but feeling you
to my core

Make-up

After touching rock bottom
the only way to go
is up
soaring
I collide into you
head-on
heart full of molten lava
kisses overturn composure
and tenderness adds touches
of charm
to thoughts
and tapestries woven
after lights
out

Ode to the Orchid

Wild and untamed
careless of convention
it rests its roots
on the bounty of chance
and scraps of fate
it sustains its blooms
on spindly stalks
tenacious tentacles
defy all odds
waving its sex
in the caress
of the breeze

The Awakening

The crypt opened
and we exhumed the mummy
silenced from serial neglect
his eyes blinked
lazily at first
then recognising kindred spirits
he smiled
they were amazed
how well he responded
to the blowing
of new life
into his stiff
joints
don't kick against the prick
he said softly
and they were surprised
by his turn of phrase
he nodded and enjoined
with quiet glee
it's a matter of chemistry
between the ears
beneath the sheets

Set Love Free

The risk he took
to open his gate
and she walked out
heart in hand
and as he waited
the clock ticked on

Bad Man, Sexy Man

The picture she paints
of the loving thug
is the most crucial
tipping point yet
all she wanted was a mother's hug
she took his love
she was fifteen
fit to smash it
into his net
for the real man was a bad man
and the bad man was sexy
he was good in bed
but after that
he was good for nothing
she closed her eyes and when she looked
she was shocked to see
he was
gone for good

Parting

Wracking nerves
they humped through hoops
and hung a noose
between careless and comical
waiting
they hatched vain plots
playing songs
out of tune
with time ticking
the cat chased the tail
reckoning the tally
of the tall order
and requiem chants
airbrushed gloom
with living colour
taking their breath away

Swinging

There they lay
in the afterglow
tantalising foreplay
followed by
good sex
and even better
was
the talk
the laughter
and
the tenderness
who would have
thunk it
worlds apart
in their beginnings
nobody knew they would
end up in love
needless to say
the parting
was raw
leaving them
both
clutching
at straws

Bare Essentials

There he stood
as naked as truth
no emperor's member
he hung his hapless staff
to dry
and as he lay in sorrow's arms
she felt dry tears
trickle
from her heart

Words out of Season

Soldering rent asunder
melting under the heat
of twisted words
strangers to mutual meanings
the mendings are askew
skies shivered
and wrapped their clouds
in safer silence
both knew the rush
of foolish feet
but still ran headlong
plying platitudes
to piece in place their
prickly fears
on the altar lie martyred musings
and love's feathers
flaying lamely
in tune with tomorrow's
timetable
all hopes now glued
to the mask
of the present
holding

Two Steps Forward

Once again we agreed
To turn over a new leaf
Write a new script
Retake the act
And while renewal
Is the middle path
And I'm thinking transformation
I am tentative
I see love beckoning
And feel the sharpness of desire
Pointing in the direction
Of secrets shared
On nocturnal sheets
And yet I hesitate
I fear
It is taking time

To stitch the wounds
That created the chasm
Between speech
And spontaneity
So now we watch warily
Circling the spots
On which we had so easily
pissed
and I am caught
in the throes of
cause and effect
ah lover
it is not an easy road
a little learning is a
dangerous thing
and the more things change
the more they remain the same

Finale

In the safety of your arms
I feel the courage
to pull the plug
on pent-up emotion
dammed by writs and rites
of propriety
it is a good thing
that you have crossed
many bridges
over many moons
and have enough
space left in your heart
for this crazy thing called
love

Twist

Ironic
oh the humour
of the universe
the joke is on me
struck by cupid
with no mercy
I blush to see truth
so naked

Chapter 5:
Existential Philosophy

Since as human beings we have the unique capacity to think and convert this skill to critical consciousness, this final chapter is devoted to reflections on life, the parts we play in this ongoing drama, speculations about the afterlife, explorations of what it all means and therefore, consideration of the metaphysical legacy we leave our progeny.

The Other Side

If we could see beyond
the veil
then mysterious bonds
between living and dead
would hold no dread
or mystery
as time bombs tick
we release our fears
and live in the moment
when time is the only
thing that is left
the beauty of silence
the charm of a smile
the caress of the breeze
magnify
the wonder of living
but cataracts have grown
on drawn blinds of souls
and blurred visions
of splendour

We Want Justice

Who guards the fortress where
rules are made
who mends them when
they are broken
whose arm is long enough
to make the laws
and make us abide
by their boundaries
I see gears shifting
and high-speed chasers
drive in reverse
psychology does a somersault dance
and if ever morality
ate at this table
it was before this age
as ground swells
and good guys go
politricks is honed to a fine hue
it's clear to see
a queen in the closet
wants a pound of flesh
for three pounds of silver
and when she clangs the gavel
on the scale
the choir will sing
farewell

Nostalgia

It used to be
that we told time
by bearings of the fruit
that time was slow
and we used to pick
ripe ones ready to eat
then there was a time
when Ancestors' arms
wrapped us in spirit
and kept us safe
from evil eye and harm
but then clocks ticking
changed all that
and lateral turned to linear
time was packaged
and defined as money
and you paid for its waste
and for capital's bounty
we race like rats
around the clock
and learn to fear the end so much
we even forget our beginning

Courage of Conviction

Salt dropped in wounds
after love's last flight
The lie in believer
the unheeded clue
slim chance band-aid
will heal the breach
gutted by passions
spent in vain
no use either
to tear flesh
off the bare bones
picking up pieces
downed in stalemate
they dumped
missed moves
and rattled on

Politically Correct

The dialectic is not romantic
and it is only in empathy
that we dare
breathe with hope
foibles of humanity
don't deserve compassion
but we give it anyway
over barriers erected
in defence of democracy
paradigms shifted
regimes changed underwear
and as freedom
waxed and waned
the caged bird sings

Outside the Box

Had to join you
and have a bash
the imagery of you
holding your phallus
and writing for dear life
was compelling
we must resist war
and environmental destruction
computers cannot compete
with auto-arousal
brain-hand union
beats
virtual reality
giving substance
to imagination

Information Age

The Dutch official assured me
it was not philanthropy
but information investment
that motivated fellowship
with four-fifths world
participants
I felt then that cerebral fruits
were children of whoredom
and policy makers
made of kindred soil
mere Bartimaeuses
of said brothels
the metaphor complete
here I am
masturbating again
in the solitude of
cryptic silence

Couplet

I longed for a fleeting look
at the moon
and yesterday
I felt my heart
in unison beat
with long-lost love
and soar
as lunar sparks flew
ignited
I withdrew
from the balcony view
satisfied

With Prejudice

He scratches the surface
and my paper-thin skin bleeds
from wellsprings
embittered by the litany
of parsimonious bureaucrats
rhetorical angst interrogated
the value added
of time in this space
till presence of mind prevailed
I was kicking ass
left right and centre
till words failed me
and pride injured
I cry
on the inside

About the Author

Dr. Imani Tafari-Ama is currently Research Fellow at the Regional Coordinating Office for the Institute for Gender and Development Studies, having completed a year as Fulbright Scholar-in-Residence at Bridgewater State University in Massachusetts. Previous to that assignment, Imani was International Fellow and Curator at the Flensburg Maritime Museum (2016-17), tasked with formulating an African-Caribbean analysis of Danish Colonialism and Legacy in Flensburg, the Virgin Islands of the United States and Ghana, culminating in the Rum, Sweat and Tears exhibition (June 2017-March 2018).

With a Ph.D. is in Development Studies and Masters degree in Women and Development Studies, Dr. Imani Tafari-Ama has lectured across a broad range of disciplines and on a number of topics including: feminist methodology/epistemology, action research and the policy process, the culture of Rastafari and African religious retentions in the Caribbean, thought and action in the African Diaspora, Dancehall, sex and religious ideology and culture and community development, as well as being invited to give special lectures on colonial history, violence and gender and development issues and Rastafari at institutions around the world.

Dr. Imani Tafari-Ama is the author of: *Blood, Bullets and Bodies: Sexual Politics Below Jamaica's Poverty Line, Up For Air: This Half Has Never Been Told* (an award-winning novel; https://youtu.be/qQNYGjRFlwk) and *Lead in the Veins* (poetry) as well as several book chapters and articles. She is also a multimedia journalist who has produced several audio-visual documentaries including 'Setting the Skin Tone', which explores the catastrophic social practice of skin bleaching (https://youtu.be/VNwIZ_xHjm0). This eight-and-a half minute video documentary (produced in 2006) is an excerpt from her Doctoral research.

www.ingramcontent.com/pod-product-compliance
Lightning Source LLC
Chambersburg PA
CBHW071315060426
42444CB00036B/3024